THE USBORNE
BOOK OF
FAMOUS
PAINTINGS

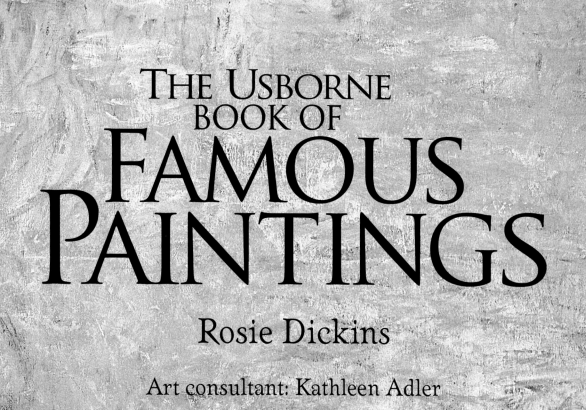

The Usborne
Book of
Famous
Paintings

Rosie Dickins

Art consultant: Kathleen Adler

Designed by Nicola Butler

With pictures by 35 famous artists
plus drawings by Philip Hopman

Contents

About this book   6-7

The Arnolfini Portrait   8-9

Spring   10-11

St. George and the Dragon   12-13

Mona Lisa   14-15

The Sistine Chapel ceiling   16-19

The Maids of Honor   20-21

The Courtyard of a House in Delft   22-23

Self Portrait   24-25

Girl with a Pearl Earring   26-27

Mr. and Mrs. Andrews   28-29

The Great Wave   30-31

The "Fighting Temeraire"   32-33

Ophelia   34-35

Dance at the Moulin de la Galette   36-37

A Bar at the Folies-Bergère   38-39

A Sunday on La Grande Jatte   40-41

Sunflowers   42-43

Blue Dancers   44-45

The Scream   46-47

The Kiss   48-49

Harmony in Red   50-51

Water Lilies, Morning   52-53

Yellow - Red - Blue   54-55

Oriental Poppies   56-57

American Gothic   58-59

The Persistence of Memory   60-61

The previous pages showed part of *Water Lilies* by Claude Monet.
You can see the whole picture by turning to page 52.
The painting on the very first page was *The Maids of Honor* by Diego Velásquez.
You can find out more about it on page 20.

Guernica   62-63

Self Portrait (The Frame)   64-65

Nighthawks   66-67

Number 6   68-69

Relativity   70-71

Golconda   72-73

Fall   74-75

Marilyn   76-77

Mr. and Mrs. Clark and Percy   78-79

Index   80

About this book

There are hundreds of famous paintings all over the world, that people recognize and admire for lots of reasons. It's impossible to say which are the best or most famous, as people will always argue about it.

For this book, we have picked a small selection of pictures – just 35, arranged in order of date – spanning a huge range of periods and styles. Looking at them may help you to discover what kind of paintings *you* like best and perhaps select your own favorites.

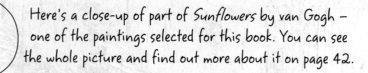

Here's a close-up of part of *Sunflowers* by van Gogh – one of the paintings selected for this book. You can see the whole picture and find out more about it on page 42.

Seeing more

Each of the paintings in this book is on display in an art gallery or museum around the world. If you visit one of those galleries, you can see the real painting for yourself. You can also view the paintings – and many, many more – on the gallery websites.

For links to the gallery websites and online art activities, go to:
www.usborne.com/quicklinks
and type in the keywords "famous paintings".
Please note, the links are regularly reviewed and updated, but Usborne Publishing is not responsible for the content of any website other than its own.

The Arnolfini Portrait

by Jan van Eyck

Belgium, 1434, oil paint on wood, 32 x 24in (82 x 60cm)

This early 15th-century portrait shows a wealthy banker, Giovanni Arnolfini, and his wife. One of the first pictures to be made with oil paints, it is amazingly lifelike. Some of the details are so tiny, the artist must have used a magnifying glass to paint them.

Wedding day?

The Arnolfinis must have been very religious because the picture is full of religious symbols. These include a set of rosary beads, used for counting prayers, beside the mirror, and a burning candle, often used to suggest God's presence, in the chandelier. Some people think the picture shows a marriage and call it *The Arnolfini Wedding*. Mr. Arnolfini solemnly raises his hand, almost as if he's taking a vow. But actually, he's probably just greeting guests.

Painting light

In the 1430s, oil paints had only just been invented — but van Eyck knew exactly how to use them. He built them up in thin, smooth layers, to create very subtle changes of color, texture and effects of light. His brushstrokes are so small and delicate, they are almost invisible.

Jan van Eyck in 1433

In this close-up of the mirror, you can see it reflects two figures entering the room. One is probably the artist himself. You can see him more clearly in his self portrait on the left.

8

Many luxurious touches show off the couple's wealth, from their fur-trimmed robes to the fancy chandelier.

The artist signed his picture on the wall above the mirror. The letters say, in Latin: *Jan van Eyck was here, 1434.*

People often think Mrs. Arnolfini looks pregnant, but that's because she's wearing a fashionably big skirt and holding it up in front of her.

Dogs are often included in pictures as symbols of love and faithfulness.

Spring

by Sandro Botticelli

Italy, about 1482, tempera paint on canvas, 6ft 8in x 10ft 4in
(2.03 x 3.14m) – making the figures nearly life-size.

This painting has fascinated viewers since it was painted over five centuries ago. Experts argue over what exactly it's supposed to mean, but they all agree on the central theme – it's a celebration of love and spring, decorated with more than 500 different plants and flowers.

Wedding picture?

The painting shows Venus, the ancient Roman goddess of love, presiding over a garden full of characters from different myths. (You can see who's who in the labels.) It was created for the powerful Medici family, by Italian artist Sandro Botticelli. Experts think it may have been a wedding gift. There was a big Medici wedding in 1492 and the picture's themes of love and new beginnings would have been perfect for the occasion.

The man with winged shoes is Mercury, the messenger of the gods. He holds up his staff to push away a rain cloud.

This trio of dancers, known as the Three Graces, represent grace and beauty.

10

Venus, goddess of love, stands in the middle with her son, Cupid, hovering above her. Cupid's arrows are said to make people fall in love.

Notice the dark frame of leaves around Venus, which makes her stand out very clearly.

The man with blue skin and billowing robes is Zephyrus, the wind of spring.

Zephyrus embraces a shy-looking nymph. His touch transforms her into Flora, goddess of flowers and spring.

Notice the flowers dropping from the nymph's lips – according to myth, this happened when she spoke.

This is Flora, goddess of flowers and spring, stepping forward and strewing roses.

St. George and the Dragon

by Raphael Sanzio (often known just as Raphael)
Italy, about 1503-05, oil paint on wood, 11 x 10in (29 x 25cm)

This dramatic, 16th-century painting illustrates a famous
story about St. George, who fought a dragon to rescue a princess.
At the time, the story was very popular with artists and their clients.
This version was probably created for an Italian nobleman.

Telling stories

The scene is full of action, with the twisting dragon and rearing
horse. George raises his arm to strike and the princess runs across
the background, her billowing dress suggesting rapid movement.
But despite the drama and speed, it's all very neatly arranged.

The misty blue
hills in the background
help to create a feeling
of distance.

This diagram
shows how the
central figures
pile up into
a pyramid.

Look for the
monstrous mix
of animal details in
the dragon, with its
spiky wings, webbed
feet and coiled,
snake-like tail.

George has already
attacked the dragon
with a lance.

There is a golden halo
around George's helmet,
to show he is a saint.

The main figures form a pyramid, with George in
the most powerful position at the top. He towers
over the dragon, his plumed helmet adding to his
height. It's easy to imagine how his sword will
come crashing down to finish off the dragon.

Bright white highlights
on George's sword and
helmet make them look
shiny and metallic.

Mona Lisa

by Leonardo da Vinci (often known just as Leonardo)
Italy, about 1505-14, oil paint on wood, 30 x 21in (77 x 53cm)

The woman in this portrait has one of the most famous faces in the world, and her picture has inspired generations of artists and writers. But no one knows for sure who she was. The most likely candidate is Lisa Giocondo, the wife of a wealthy Italian merchant.

Mystery smile

Lisa's strange half-smile is what fascinates people. Is she happy, sad or simply bored? Her expression is impossible to pin down, and seems to change depending on the angle you look at it. Leonardo used a technique known as *sfumato* to create this effect, deliberately blurring the corners of her mouth and eyes.

This close-up shows the soft, blurred shadows at the corners of her mouth. It also reveals how the surface of the paint has cracked over time.

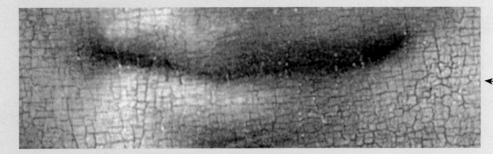

Stolen art

Leonardo spent years perfecting the picture – x-rays reveal three earlier versions below the surface. He eventually gave it to the King of France, who hung it in his bathroom. Later, it was given to a Paris museum. In 1911, the picture hit headlines when it was stolen by a workman who wanted to take it back to Italy. After two years, it was discovered inside a false-bottomed trunk and returned to Paris, where it is seen by millions each year.

Notice the gauzy veil over her hair.

Lisa's missing eyebrows look strange nowadays. But, in her day, it was fashionable for women to pluck or shave them.

Notice how the landscape turns hazy and blue in the distance. This effect is known as aerial perspective, and it helps to give the painting a feeling of depth.

You can see Leonardo's amazing attention to detail in the delicate embroidery on the dress.

15

The Sistine Chapel ceiling

by Michelangelo Buonarroti (often known just as Michelangelo)
Italy, 1508-12, fresco (watercolor paint on plaster), 46 x 133ft (13.2 x 40.5m)

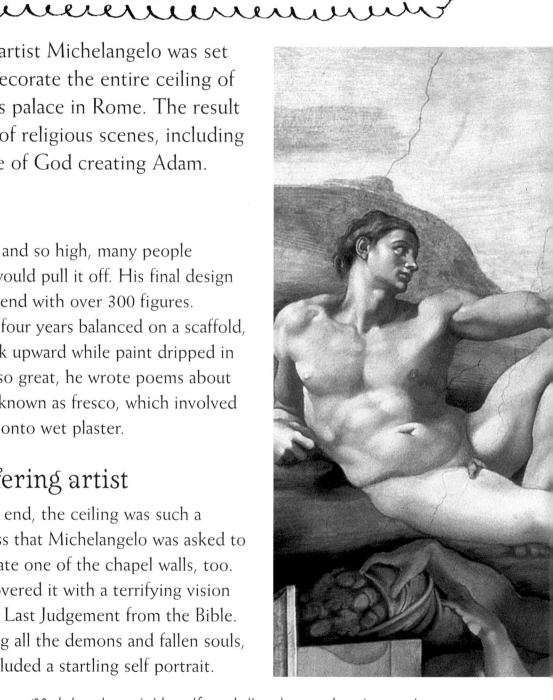

Five centuries ago, artist Michelangelo was set a big challenge: to decorate the entire ceiling of a chapel in the pope's palace in Rome. The result was a stunning series of religious scenes, including this famous image of God creating Adam.

A tall order

The ceiling was so huge and so high, many people doubted Michelangelo would pull it off. His final design filled the ceiling end-to-end with over 300 figures. To paint them, he spent four years balanced on a scaffold, painfully craning his neck upward while paint dripped in his face. The strain was so great, he wrote poems about it. He used a technique known as fresco, which involved brushing colors directly onto wet plaster.

Suffering artist

In the end, the ceiling was such a success that Michelangelo was asked to decorate one of the chapel walls, too. He covered it with a terrifying vision of the Last Judgement from the Bible. Among all the demons and fallen souls, he included a startling self portrait.

Michelangelo painted himself as a hollow skin — perhaps to remind viewers of the suffering he endured while decorating the chapel.

You can see more of the ceiling on the next page.

Notice the tiny gap between God's finger and Adam's, which adds to the drama of the moment.

The lifelike, muscular bodies reveal Michelangelo's skill in anatomy – something he probably learned from dissecting dead bodies.

The ceiling is a dizzying 66ft (20m) above the ground.
Strong colors and clear outlines make it easier to see the figures from the floor.

The Maids of Honor

by Diego Velázquez

Spain, 1656, oil paint on canvas, 10ft 5in x 9ft 1in (3.18 x 2.76m) – making the picture itself about lifesize.

This unusual portrait gives you a peek at royal life behind the scenes. It shows a young Spanish princess, Margarita, surrounded by the everyday bustle of courtiers and servants – including the artist himself. "Maids of Honor" (in Spanish, *Las Meninas*) are the Queen's personal attendants.

Look for touches of red across the picture. There is a red cup being offered to the princess on a golden tray.

There is also a red cross on the artist's chest; this was probably added a few years later, to commemorate an award the King gave him.

Mirror image

At first glance, the princess seems to be the focus of attention. The other figures are neatly arranged around her, and the shadowy background shows off her pale, pretty hair and dress perfectly. But if you study their faces, she and several others are gazing out of the picture at something. What is it?

The answer lies in the mirror on the wall behind. It reveals a couple overlooking the scene – the King and Queen. King Philip disliked having his portrait painted as he grew older, but the artist cleverly found this way of including him anyway, creating a portrait not just of the princess, but of her parents too.

A little courtier dressed in red tries to rouse a sleeping dog with his foot.

Although it's still hazy, you can see the reflection of the King and Queen, standing under a red curtain, more clearly in this close-up.

The Courtyard of a House in Delft

by Pieter de Hooch
Netherlands, 1658, oil paint on canvas, 29 x 24in (74 x 60cm)

This 350-year-old picture shows an everyday household scene in the Dutch town of Delft. Two women and a child stand in an exquisitely detailed setting of weathered brick, worn wood and rambling plants, all delicately colored with a soft, afternoon light.

See how the light from the street forms a halo around the woman in the house.

Look for the artist's initials, carved into a stone at the base of the doorway.

Home sweet home?

When this picture was made, there was a fashion for domestic scenes. Some people think the painting celebrates the pleasures of a well-kept home, with its neatly swept yard, well-tended plants and happy-looking mother and child. But others feel it suggests the confinement of home life, with the woman in the corridor gazing longingly at the street, as if dreaming of the world beyond.

Notice how the striped arch is repeated in the distance.

Tricking the eye

The picture looks amazingly lifelike – although the buildings it shows only existed in the artist's imagination. Neat lines of receding bricks, and a tantalizing glimpse through a corridor, create a strong sense of space and depth. The artist used a technique known as perspective to create an accurate illusion of real, 3-D space on his flat, 2-D canvas.

This diagram shows the use of perspective. The rules of perspective say that parallel lines (shown here in blue) seem to get closer as they get farther away, until they meet at the horizon (shown in green).

Self Portrait

by Rembrandt van Rijn
Netherlands, 1661, oil paint on canvas, 45 x 37in (114 x 94cm)

Rembrandt van Rijn painted himself over 40 times during his life,
creating one of the most remarkable series of self portraits ever made.
This version shows him at the age of 55, looking old and careworn,
but displaying his palette and brushes with quiet pride.

An honest look

Look for the artist's tools – a rectangular palette, brushes and long "mahl stick," which Rembrandt used to steady his hand while painting.

This is a plain, unfussy portrait, painted in muted colors. Rembrandt shows himself in his everyday work clothes – a painter's cap and warm housecoat. And he's not afraid to record unflattering lines and wrinkles. The background is equally plain, decorated only by two mysterious circles. They might be hemispheres on an unfinished map, or they might refer to a story about an earlier artist, Giotto. According to the story, when Giotto was asked to prove his skill, he painted a perfect circle.

Notice how light catches the cap and face, focusing our attention there, while the bottom of the picture is lost in shadows.

Streaks and daubs

In this detail, you can see the thick paint used to build up the eyes, helping to add character to the portrait.

Up close, the picture dissolves into rough streaks and daubs of paint. Look at the hand holding the palette – you can hardly make out the fingers. But if you step back, the marks all merge to form a surprisingly natural portrait.

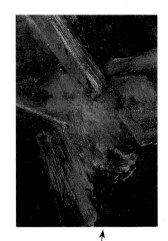

This is a close up of the hand.
Notice how the fingers are just a few hasty dashes.

Girl with a Pearl Earring

by Jan Vermeer

Netherlands, about 1665-75, oil paint on canvas, 18 x 15in (45 x 39cm)

This beautiful picture was painted about 350 years ago.
But it was lost for over 200 years, and only became famous after
a collector rediscovered it. It has since inspired a well-known novel
and movie. The girl's name is not known, but the artist, Jan Vermeer,
skillfully suggests her lively expression and exotic clothes.

Mystery picture

People often speculate about the girl's identity. You can't tell from her clothes – the silky turban and pearl earring are just for dress-up. She might have been Vermeer's daughter or maid. The artist was probably more interested in studying her costume and expression than in making her portrait. Such studies, known as "tronies" in the Netherlands, were very popular at the time.

The painting is so smooth and lifelike, it almost looks like a photograph. Vermeer blended his brushstrokes until they were nearly invisible. He may also have used a kind of early camera, known as a "camera obscura," to help him draw. This projects an image into a darkened room, so the artist can copy it.

An image made with a camera obscura tends to have soft outlines and bright spots of light, which is just how Vermeer painted his picture – as you can see in this detail.

Notice the girl's natural pose, as if she's just glancing over her shoulder.

See how the plain, dark background and slanting light focus attention on her face.

Close up, you can see that the brilliant shine on the pearl is really a thick smear of white.

The silky turban was painted using ultramarine blue — an expensive color made from crushed lapis lazuli, which is a semi-precious stone.

Look for gleaming highlights on the eyes and lips, which bring the face to life.

By contrast, the line of the nose almost disappears in the light.

The background was originally dark green, but has blackened over time.

Mr. and Mrs. Andrews

by Thomas Gainsborough
England, about 1750, oil paint on canvas, 28 x 47in (70 x 119cm)

Look for the unfinished patch on Mrs. Andrews' lap. It was meant to be filled in later – perhaps with a bird shot by her husband, or a portrait of a hoped-for child.

Notice the detail on the clothes, from Mr. Andrews' rumpled coat and wrinkled stockings, to his wife's silky skirts and dainty slippers. The artist probably arranged the clothes on mannequins in his studio, so he could take his time painting them.

This 18th-century portrait shows newlyweds Robert and Frances Andrews on their country estate. They are dressed to impress, in expensive clothes. But what really dominates the picture is the glowing English landscape.

People and places

At first sight, the portrait seems to reflect the pride of a wealthy, land-owning couple, as they survey their well-kept fields. But they don't look very at home in the setting. Their stiff poses and fashionable clothes are at odds with the rural surroundings. And the landscape takes pride of place, with the couple pushed to one side – a very unusual, off-center arrangement.

The artist, Thomas Gainsborough, was a successful portrait artist, but was often impatient with his rich clients. He said he preferred painting landscapes. Back then, it was rare to include a real landscape in a portrait – the fashion was to show idealized, imaginary backgrounds. But here, Gainsborough had the chance to paint a real place that he knew well. The Andrews' estate lay close to his childhood home, and he captured the familiar countryside in loving detail.

Close up, you can make out a tower beyond the trees in the middle of the scene. It belongs to All Saints Church, near Gainsborough's hometown of Sudbury, and it still stands today.

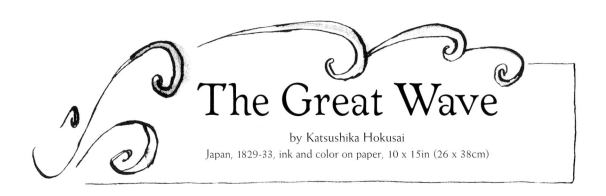

The Great Wave

by Katsushika Hokusai

Japan, 1829-33, ink and color on paper, 10 x 15in (26 x 38cm)

Made nearly 200 years ago, this dramatic scene shows a huge wave about to crash over three tiny boats, with Japan's Mount Fuji just visible in the distance. A print rather than a painting, it has become one of the best-known examples of Japanese art.

Printed picture

The picture first appeared as part of a series of views of Mount Fuji. It was printed using carved wooden blocks – one block for each color. One by one, the blocks were coated with ink, and paper was pressed onto them, to build up the final image. Because it was a print, the artist could make and sell lots of copies cheaply. This print proved so popular, the blocks used to make it wore out.

You can see how each patch of color has clear edges, and the white foam has been turned into menacing claws.

Making waves

The wave towers over everything else in the picture, even the peak of Mount Fuji. The low horizon line helps make the wave seem even bigger. It makes you feel as if you're down among the waves, along with the sailors, as they fight this great force of nature in their little wooden boats.

The artist wrote the picture title in a box and signed his name beside it.

Notice how the waves curve around and frame Mount Fuji – and how the shape and color of the snowy mountain is echoed by the foamy swell.

The white areas were created by letting the white of the paper show through.

The printing process restricted the number of colors and shades that could be used – this print contains just seven. Bold stripes of a color known as "Berlin blue" were used to create the water, sailors and mountain.

The "Fighting Temeraire"

by J.M.W. Turner

England, 1839, oil paint on canvas, 36 x 48in (91 x 122cm)

This atmospheric scene records the final voyage of an old warship, the *Temeraire*, on its way to be broken up for scrap. It was painted in England over 150 years ago by J.M.W. Turner. When the picture was exhibited, it was an instant hit. The picture was also one of Turner's favorites. He called it his "darling" and refused to sell it. When he died, he left it to the British nation. It has been on public display ever since.

Look for more sailing ships in the distance beyond the *Temeraire*, including a tall ship with its sails unfurled – like the ghost of the *Temeraire* in her glory.

The picture's full title is:

The "Fighting Temeraire" Being Tugged to her Last Berth to be Broken Up, 1838

Fact and fiction

Turner was on the spot sketching when the *Temeraire* was towed away by a pair of steam tugs, already minus her masts and guns, early one morning. But when the artist came to paint the scene in his studio, he decided to change things around. He removed one tug and put back the masts, exaggerating the contrast between the tall, elegant sailing ship and the squat, steam-belching tug.

End of an era

Turner also changed the time of day, adding a dramatic sunset, to conjure up a feeling of ending and loss. And it's not just about the loss of one ship. At the time, Britain's naval power was waning and steam engines were starting to replace old forms of transportation, such as sailing ships. So the painting is more than a record of one event – it's an image of changing times.

Notice how the blazing clouds are painted with rough smears of orange and yellow.

More orangish-yellow smears capture the reflections of the sunset on the water.

Ophelia

by John Millais

England, 1851-52, oil paint on canvas, 30 x 44in (76 x 112cm)

This beautifully detailed painting illustrates a scene from Shakespeare's famous play, *Hamlet*. In the play, Ophelia goes insane with grief after the death of her father and drowns while picking flowers. Almost all the flowers here are mentioned in the play.

Suffering for art

The artist, John Millais, wanted his picture to look as lifelike as possible. So he spent months painting a real English riverbank, braving bad weather and being bitten by flies. But he went back to his studio to paint Ophelia. He hired a model named Lizzie Siddal, gave her an antique dress and got her to lie in a bathtub for hours – until the water got chilly and Lizzie caught a terrible cold.

Look for a robin perching on the willow branches. Ophelia mentions a robin in the play.

The yellowish patches in the reeds are caused by some of the original paint fading over the years.

Notice all the different kinds of leaves in the background,
and how the falling light turns them different shades of green.

Millais used thin layers of paint
on top of a layer of white, to make
his colors look bright and sharp.
X-rays show he made hardly
any changes as he painted.

Ophelia is surrounded
by plants with symbolic
meanings. Some of
the meanings are
listed here:
• weeping willow — sadness
• nettles — pain
• roses — love and beauty
• pansies — thoughts
• forget-me-nots — memory
• daisies — innocence
• poppies and violets
— death.

Can you spot a
skull-like shape among
the leaves on the bank?
It could be an accidental
effect of the shadows,
or a deliberate omen
of death.

Millais originally planned to include a water vole swimming in the river,
but left it out after a friend's uncle mistook his sketch for a rabbit.

36   The nearest dancers are an artist named
Cardenas and a model named Margot.

Renoir persuaded a local girl named
Estelle to pose for him in her striped dress.

Dance at the Moulin de la Galette

by Auguste Renoir
France, 1876, oil paint on canvas, 4ft 4in x 5ft 9in (1.31 x 1.75m)

Painted over 100 years ago, this picture shows a buzzing crowd enjoying themselves at a Paris dancehall known as the *Moulin de la Galette*. The artist, Auguste Renoir, lived nearby and asked many of his friends to pose for him.

Notice how the scene shimmers with light and color. The ground is a dazzling white, and even the shadows are painted in blue, rather than black.

Look for the clever arrangement of figures. At first glance, it seems like a casual snapshot. But everyone was carefully placed so most of Renoir's friends face the viewer.

Bright and blurry

Renoir made frequent visits to the dancehall, to make sketches of the open-air dancefloor and plan his picture. He wanted to show the place at its sunniest and best, with everyone in their finest clothes. You can see how his light, feathery brushstrokes make everything look soft and pretty.

Today, the picture is considered a masterpiece, but when it was first exhibited, most viewers hated it. With its glowing colors and blurry brushmarks, they thought it looked garish and unfinished. But for Renoir, it was about capturing an on-the-spot impression of light and movement.

The two men sitting facing us are Norbert and Georges, close friends of Renoir's.

A Bar at the Folies-Bergère

by Édouard Manet

France, 1882, oil paint on canvas, 38 x 51in (96 x 130cm)

Notice the green boots here. They belong to an acrobat on a trapeze, high above the crowd.

The artist signed his name on the label of this bottle.

This painting offers a glittering glimpse of a busy bar in 19th-century Paris. The scene is cleverly arranged so most of it is seen in the mirror behind the bar. It's as if you are standing right there, facing the wistful-looking barmaid.

A vase of roses adds a touch of softness amid all the marble and glass.

Look for the mirror's golden frame. Notice how the mirror glass is misted with blue, too.

The figures in the background were dashed in with rapid, blurry strokes, suggesting a fidgety crowd.

Nights out

The Folies-Bergère was a popular evening spot where people could go to drink and watch entertainers, including musicians, dancers and circus acts. The artist, Édouard Manet, made sketches in the Folies, but worked on the painting in his studio, hiring a real Folies barmaid, named Suzon, to pose for him.

Puzzling picture

There is something strange about the mirror. If you look closely, Suzon and some of the bottles don't match their reflections. X-rays show Manet altered the reflection, probably to avoid cluttering the background. The man in the top hat is another puzzle. The reflection shows him standing just in front of Suzon – where you, the viewer, ought to be. It's as if you've been turned into a 19th-century gentleman and included in the scene.

A Sunday on La Grande Jatte

by Georges Seurat

France, 1884-86, oil paint on canvas, 6ft 10in x 10ft 1in (2.08 x 3.08m)

French artist Georges Seurat spent
two years on this shimmering park scene.
He made dozens of sketches before starting
a huge canvas, which he covered in tiny
dots, dabs and dashes of color –
about 3.5 million of them.

Going dotty

Seurat arranged his dots following 19th-century
theories about how we perceive color. If you
look closely, you see lots of separate colored dots
and dashes. But, from a distance, they blur and the
colors seem to mix. Seurat thought that
because the mixing happens directly
in your eye, the results should be
brighter and richer.

Seurat also exploited the way
colors work together, adding
touches of different colors to
create zingy contrasts. So the
blue water sparkles with touches
of orange, and the green grass glows
against patches of reddish-brown.

You can see the dots and dashes
more clearly in this close-up.

40

Notice the different boats on the river, including steam tugs, sailing yachts and row boats.

The picture is very cleverly arranged, almost like a stage set. The figures have all been placed at precise distances from each other, and the areas of light and dark have been carefully balanced.

Seurat said he wanted to paint "modern people" and included a wide range – from men in top hats to workers in shirtsleeves, and from women fishing to a man playing a bugle.

The light areas are speckled with sunny oranges and yellows.

The shadows are dotted with dark blues and purples.

Look for a tiny orange butterfly hovering over the grass.

This woman is taking a pet monkey for a walk.

41

Sunflowers

by Vincent van Gogh

Netherlands, late 1888 or early 1889, oil paint on canvas, 36 x 28in (92 x 71cm)

In the late 1880s, Dutch artist Vincent van Gogh began a series of dazzling yellow sunflower paintings. These became some of van Gogh's favorite works. Despite remaining unsold during his lifetime, they are now among the most sought-after and valuable paintings in the world.

Sunshine and flowers

Each flower is a burst of intensely colored, thickly layered paint, set off by a contrasting blue-gray background. The petals were painted with thick streaks of a new chemical-based color known as chrome yellow. For van Gogh, this sunny golden yellow was a symbol of friendship and happiness. But the painting also hints at how fragile life is, as some of the flowers are starting to droop and wither.

Ups and downs

Van Gogh painted the sunflowers for a friend, Paul Gauguin, who was coming to stay. But after a few weeks, they began to fight. Van Gogh, who suffered from mental illness, seized a blade and cut off part of his own ear. Gauguin fled. Van Gogh painted the self portrait on the right while recovering.

Look for the thick, bumpy layers of paint, known as *impasto*. They are so thick, you can still see the ridges left by the brush.

The artist signed his name on the vase.

Self Portrait with Bandaged Ear, 1889

44

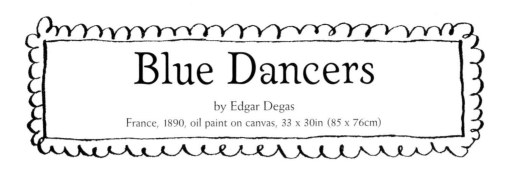

Blue Dancers

by Edgar Degas
France, 1890, oil paint on canvas, 33 x 30in (85 x 76cm)

This painting shows a group of dancers – not dancing, as you might expect, but getting ready to go on stage. It's like a casual snapshot of theater life, with the dancers crowded together, adjusting their costumes and warming up, apparently unaware of being watched.

See how scenery blocks part of the view, adding to the casual feel.

Notice how the dancers turn away, as if oblivious to the artist's gaze.

Drawing with color

The dancers are a mass of shimmering blue, surrounded by smudged pieces of scenery. Everything is built up out of dabs and dashes of color, rather than clear shapes and lines. The artist, Edgar Degas, called his method "drawing with color." The soft, hazy effect conjures up a magical atmosphere.

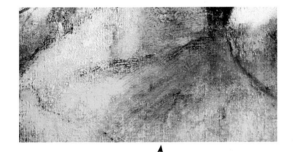

The use of contrasting colors also helps to focus your gaze and give a feeling of depth. In the middle of all the blues, a patch of bright yellowy orange stands out strongly, helping to draw your eye toward the figures in the background.

You can see the rough, smeary brushstrokes more clearly in this close-up.

Many dancers

The picture may look swift and sketchy, but the skill and observation that went into making it were the result of many years' study. During his life, Degas painted and sculpted hundreds of dancers. He was fascinated by how they moved, their grace and strength – and he felt the way they practiced, with lots of repeated exercises, was similar to the way an artist works.

45

The Scream

by Edvard Munch

Norway, 1893, oil and tempera paints and pastel on cardboard, 36 x 29in (91 x 74cm)

This dizzying, nightmare scene was created just over a century ago by Norwegian artist, Edvard Munch. An intense, powerful image of a lonely, suffering figure, it has helped to inspire everything from cartoons to horror movies.

Life scenes

Munch made several versions of the picture, both in color and black-and-white. They formed part of a series called *The Frieze of Life*, which explored life, love, death and the intense feelings these can arouse. Munch spent years on the series, rearranging and adding new pictures.

Notice the jarring clash between the orangish-red sky and blue-black water.

See how the figure's head is shaped like a skull.

The distant people contrast with the figure and make him appear more isolated.

The bridge slices sharply across the scene, trapping the figure in a narrow, uncomfortable space.

Whose scream?

The figure's mouth gapes, as if he is screaming, so you might think the picture title refers to him. But Munch said his inspiration really came from a scream he felt, mysteriously, in the world around him. He described the moment in his diary:

I was walking along the road with two friends. The sun was setting... Suddenly the sky turned blood-red. I stopped... My friends walked on – I stood there, trembling with fear. And I sensed a great, infinite scream pass through nature.

Strange, swirling lines suggest the echoes of this terrifying noise.

47

The Kiss

by Gustav Klimt

Austria, 1907-08, oil paint, gold and silver leaf on canvas, 5ft 11in x 5ft 11in (1.8 x 1.8m)

This glittering, golden image of a man kissing a woman was created 100 years ago by Gustav Klimt. Klimt's art was often controversial, but *The Kiss* was an instant hit.

Perfect patterns

When you look at the couple, only their heads, hands and feet stand out — the rest is a sumptuous swirl of shape and color. Different patterns define each of their bodies, but the patterns overlap and mingle, symbolizing their togetherness. The effect is rich and decorative, rather like a mosaic. The man and woman kneel on a carpet of bright, jewel-like flowers, but the background is plain and empty. The lack of a specific setting makes it feel as if the picture could come from any time or place.

Pure gold

The picture was painted in oils and coated with paper-thin pieces of gold and silver leaf. Klimt used so much gold in his pictures at this time, it has been called his golden period. Here, the gold surrounds the two people, giving them a magical, shimmering aura.

Close up, you can see how Klimt scraped decorative swirls and curls on top of the gold. The lines catch the light in different ways, adding to the magical effect.

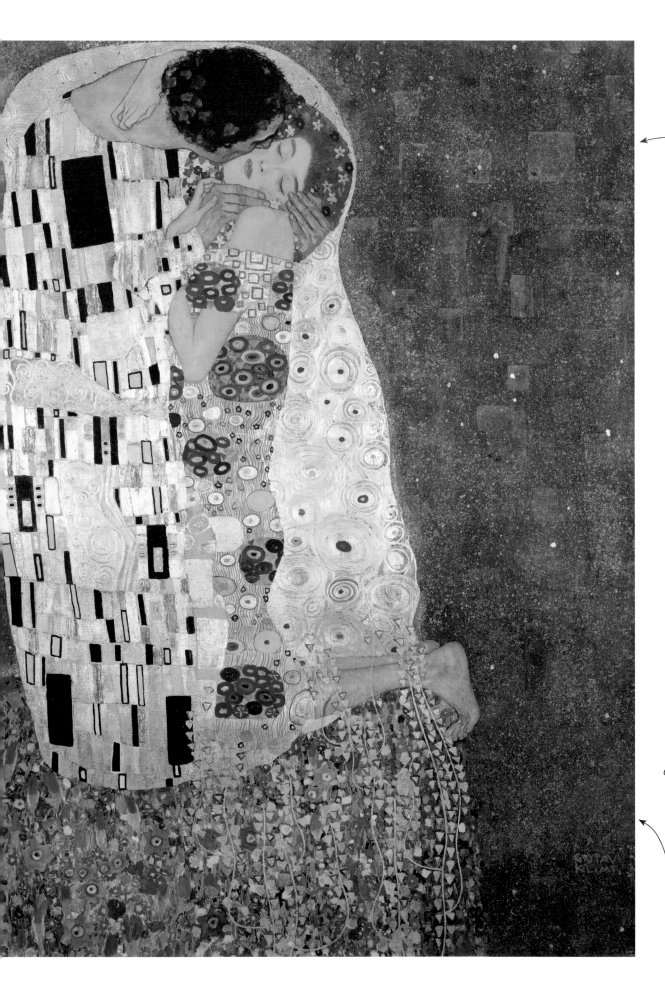

The man wears an ivy wreath, and the woman has flowers in her hair.

Notice the contrasting patterns on the couple's clothes: black-and-white blocks on the man's; bright circles of flowers on the woman's.

The woman is also wrapped in a long, embroidered cloak or veil, which cascades down her back. The bottom of it is transparent, but you can see the lines of embroidery draped over her legs.

Harmony in Red

by Henri Matisse

France, 1908, oil paint on canvas, 5ft 11in x 7ft 3in (1.81 x 2.21m)

This bright, patterned picture shows a woman setting a table with fruit and drink. But it's really as much about pattern and color, and the illusion of painting a "real" scene, as it is about the scene itself.

Seeing red

The picture began life as *Harmony in Blue,* with a blue tablecloth and wallpaper. But then the artist changed his mind and painted over them to create *Harmony in Red.* The blue picture had already been sold – but luckily the buyer, an enthusiastic Russian collector, didn't mind the change.

The real deal?

The artist, Henri Matisse, played a game with the landscape in the background. Is it meant to be a "real" view through a window, or a picture hanging on the wall? Matisse left it deliberately unclear – a reminder that the whole painting is no more "real" than this tantalizing landscape.

Notice how the landscape is painted in cool blues and greens, helping to balance the bold, bright interior.

The furniture is cut off at the edges, making the scene feel tightly enclosed.

The rich, glowing red conjures up a feeling of warmth and creates vibrant contrasts with the blues and yellows.

50

Are these orangish-yellow strips part of a window recess, or part of a picture frame? It's a deliberate puzzle, with no right or wrong answer.

The same blue pattern covers both wallpaper and tablecloth, making the table seem as flat as the walls.

Look for the way the curved shapes of the pattern are echoed by the curved shapes of the fruit, flowers and trees, and of the woman's hair.

Water Lilies, Morning

by Claude Monet

France, 1914-18, oil paint on four canvas panels, 6ft 7in x 41ft 10in (2 x 12.75m) in total

French artist Claude Monet devoted the last 30 years
of his life to water lilies. He built a huge lily pond in his garden,
and painted it again and again, at all times of day, to try to capture
the changing effect of sunlight on the flowers and water.

Bold impressions

This picture shows the pond in the soft light of morning. Painted with
loose, swirling brushstrokes, and streaks and dabs of unblended color,
it creates a bold impression – so bold, you might not even realize it's a lily
pond at first. It's painted on a vast scale, and the pond seems even bigger
because Monet left out the edges, as if the water stretched on forever.

Open out the page to see the whole painting.

Monet's garden

Monet created a spectacular garden at his home in Giverny, France. Over the years, it became as much a work of art as the paintings he made of it. He planted dazzling displays of colorful flowers and unusual plants. And for the pond, he got permission to dam a river – despite opposition from farmers, who feared his lilies would clog up the water. Today, the garden is open to the public and attracts thousands of visitors.

Over part of the pond, Monet built a Japanese-style bridge, which he also included in some of his paintings.

True to life

If you compare this photograph to Monet's painting, you can see how truthfully he painted it, despite the sketchiness of his style. The calm water mirrors the surrounding plants and sky, interrupted only by floating lilies.
In the background, a fringe of reeds and wall of trees obscure the water's edge and the horizon beyond.

This photograph shows the pond today. You can just see the Japanese bridge in the distance.

Notice how the surface of the water changes color, suggesting reflections of plants and trees, and a blue sky with clouds overhead.

Look for the way plants and water fill the entire canvas, leaving no solid ground.

Peaceful picture

This gigantic picture is one of a series showing the lily pond from dawn to dusk. Monet created the series during the First World War, perhaps as an escape from the horrors of the times. The day after the war ended, he gave the series to the French nation – a set of peaceful landscapes, to commemorate the new peace. The paintings now hang in a specially built gallery in Paris.

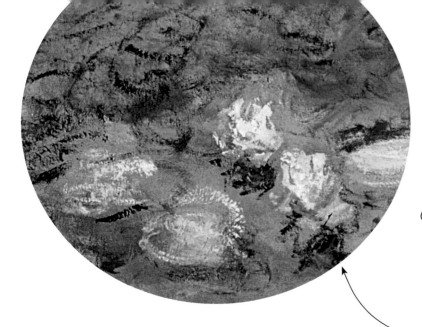

Close up, the lilies dissolve into colored blobs.

Loose, wavy brushstrokes suggest rippling water, interrupted by patches of lilies.

The lily canvases were so big, Monet had to build a special studio in his garden to put them in.

Yellow - Red - Blue

by Wassily Kandinsky

Russia, 1925, oil paint on canvas, 4ft 2in x 6ft 7in (1.27 x 2m)

To many people, some of these shapes suggest objects.
See if you can make out a face in profile, a yellow lighthouse and a waving flag.

This 1920s picture is crowded with bright shapes, but what's it all about? The title is just a list of colors. It's a clue this isn't meant to be any kind of real-life scene, but an "abstract" arrangement of shapes and colors.

Seeing shapes

The artist, Wassily Kandinsky, believed looking at shapes and colors could make you feel emotions, similar to when you listen to music. (He was a gifted musician and often compared painting to music.) This painting is built around three bright geometric shapes – a yellow rectangle, red cross and blue circle. To Kandinsky, the circle was a symbol of the human soul. Smaller shapes and lines are layered over the top, creating dramatic contrasts of form and angle.

Colorful ideas

Yellow, red and blue are known as the "primary" colors – meaning the colors from which all other shades can be mixed. They also had important symbolic values for Kandinsky...

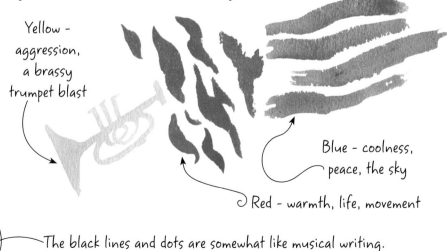

Yellow - aggression, a brassy trumpet blast

Blue - coolness, peace, the sky

Red - warmth, life, movement

The black lines and dots are somewhat like musical writing.

Notice the feeling of movement created by the mix of colors and shapes. The contrasts encourage your eyes to keep glancing around the picture.

Oriental Poppies

by Georgia O'Keeffe
America, 1927, oil paint on canvas, 30 x 40in (76 x 102cm)

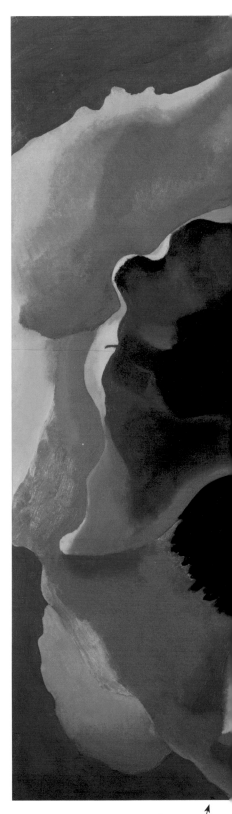

This rich red painting was created by American artist, Georgia O'Keeffe. She enlarged two poppies to about ten times their actual size, so their silky petals fill a whole canvas – creating a big, lasting record of these small, short-lived flowers.

Just flowers?

The poppies were painted with great detail and precision. But there are no leaves or stems, and no hint of where they are. There are only the flowers, a display of glowing reds and velvety blacks, set against a plain red background. Poppies are a common plant, but this intense focus invites you to look at them in a new way. Painted like this, they begin to seem less like flowers, and more like a way of exploring abstract shapes and colors.

Taking time

Of her intention, O'Keeffe said: "Nobody takes time to see a flower, really, it is so small. We haven't time and to see takes time... So I said to myself: I'll paint what I see... what the flower is to me – but I'll paint it big... I'll make even busy New Yorkers take time to see what I see of flowers."

Look for all the tints of red, from scarlet to pink and orange.

56

Notice the flat, almost photographic finish — the result of thousands
of tiny brushstrokes, over a specially prepared, super-smooth canvas.

American Gothic

by Grant Wood
America, 1930, oil paint on board, 31 x 26in (78 x 65cm)

This picture of American country folk won a prize for its creator,
Grant Wood, when it first went on show in Chicago in 1930.
Since then, it has inspired endless copies and spoofs, and
is often claimed to be America's most famous painting.

Home sweet home

Notice how the man and woman block our way, and the windows of the house are covered. This is a closed-off, private world.

The picture was inspired by a house – a real cottage in Eldon, Iowa – which you can see in this photograph. The arched "Gothic" style window on the top floor gave the painting its title. For the couple, Wood persuaded his dentist and sister to dress up as farmers, saying they were, "the kind of people I fancied should live in that house." Double portraits are often used for pictures of husband and wife. But here the man is so much older, many people think they are father and daughter.

The house is now a center devoted to the painting.

Satire or celebration?

There is a hint of threat in the pitchfork. Look for echoes of its shape in the lines of the man's overalls and on his chin.

The woman's hair is tied severely back, but a loose curl suggests she has a gentler side.

When the picture was put on show, it divided public opinion. Some people complained Wood was poking fun at farmers by making them look dour and old-fashioned. But others claimed the picture celebrated farmers' strength and hard-work. Wood himself refused to comment, saying only: "These are types of people I have known all my life. I tried to characterize them truthfully – to make them more like themselves than they were in actual life."

The Persistence of Memory

by Salvador Dalí

Spain, 1931, oil paint on canvas, 10 x 13in (24 x 33cm) – no bigger than many photographs.

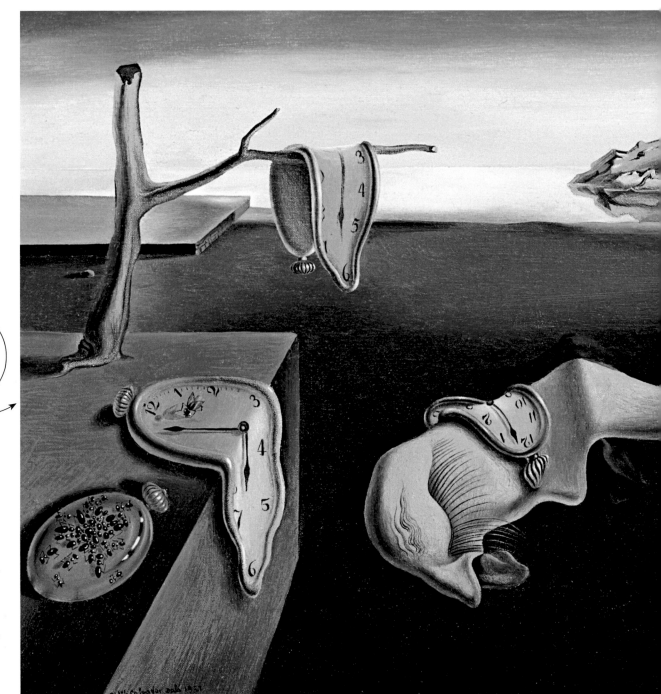

Notice how the watch faces all show different times.

A fly crawls over one watch.

Ants cluster on the case of another watch.

The dead tree, ants and fly are all symbols of decay. As a child, Dalí had an intense fear of ants.

The strange, sleeping figure is actually a distorted version of Dalí's own profile.

This weird landscape, with its droopy watches, looks like something out of a dream – which is exactly what the artist, Salvador Dalí, intended. He believed dreams reveal our unconscious thoughts, and can be in some ways more "real" than reality.

Time and memory

The painting is full of mysterious symbols. A lifeless tree and a sleeping figure suggest death and dreams. Watches and sand are traditionally used to represent time. But these watches are melting or being eaten by ants, as if time is breaking down and losing its meaning. However the title seems to say that memory persists, regardless of time – and the picture conjures up two of Dalí's own childhood memories: cliffs and ants.

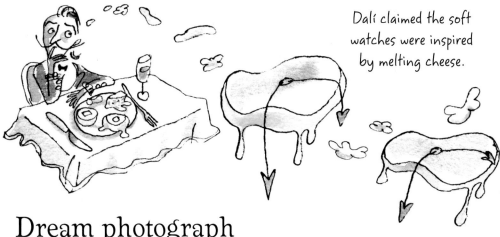

Dalí claimed the soft watches were inspired by melting cheese.

Dream photograph

Despite all the strange things in the picture, the polished brushwork and lifelike use of light and shadows are designed to make it seem as real as possible. Dalí described his works as "hand-painted dream photographs." The picture's first owner described it as "Dalí dynamite!" When it was first exhibited, it created a sensation, and was rapidly snapped up by a major New York museum.

The golden cliffs were based on a place in Spain, near Dalí's childhood home.

Guernica

by Pablo Picasso
Spain, 1937, oil paint on canvas, 3.49 x 7.77m (11ft 6in x 25ft 6in)

Spanish artist Pablo Picasso created this
powerful anti-war painting to protest against
a horrific event during the Spanish
Civil War. In 1937, hundreds of civilians
died in the Spanish town of Guernica after
it was pounded by bomber planes.

What's in the picture?

A bull watches a woman clutch a dead child.
According to Picasso, the bull represented
"brutality and darkness".

A woman falls from
a burning house.

Picasso said the horse stood for "the people".
Its side has been pierced by a spear.

A dead soldier lies on the ground.

A woman
tries to flee.

From a window,
a face looks on in horror.

62

Open out the page to see the whole painting.

In the news

The attack on Guernica was headline news. Bleak, black-and-white images of the devastation were screened in movie newsreels and printed in newspapers. Picasso saw these images, and echoed them by choosing to paint his picture in stark black and white.

Propaganda picture

In making the picture, Picasso said he felt "a deliberate sense of propaganda." Through it, he hoped to raise awareness and rally opposition to the extreme right-wing forces behind the bombing. The painting's huge size and tortured figures were designed to have the maximum impact.

The incident was condemned around the world, but that didn't help Spain. The war ended with the country in the grip of a brutal dictatorship. Picasso refused to let *Guernica* be seen in Spain until democracy was restored – which finally happened in 1975. Today, the painting lives in Madrid.

This photograph shows Guernica just after the bombing. The town center was reduced to rubble, with fires that burned for three days. A third of the town's inhabitants were killed or injured.

Look for the jagged, distorted shapes, which make everything seem twisted and broken.

Notice the abrupt changes between light and dark, which suggest the flashes of exploding bombs.

The picture was so big, it barely fit in Picasso's studio.

Self Portrait (The Frame)

by Frida Kahlo

Mexico, 1938, oil paint on metal with glass, 11 x 8in (29 x 21cm)

The face looking out of this cheerfully colored frame is that of
Mexican artist, Frida Kahlo. Kahlo turned to art while recovering
from a crippling traffic accident, and painted herself over
100 times, saying she was the subject she knew best.

Mexican art

The picture celebrates Kahlo's Mexican roots. The decorations
were inspired by Mexican folk art, and the portrait itself shows
Kahlo in traditional Mexican costume, with ribbons and flowers
in her hair. The painting was exhibited in a show of Mexican
art and became an instant success when it was bought by the
famous Louvre Museum in Paris.

Notice all the different
flowers and decorative shapes
which make up the frame.

Look for the mix
of styles. The frame is
deliberately bold, bright
and simple. By contrast,
Kahlo's face is more lifelike.

You can see how a solid
patch of blue surrounds her
face, making it stand out
from the decorations.

The birds may have been
based on Kahlo's pets.
She kept many animals,
including parrots and
monkeys, and often
included them in
her portraits.

Look for two
exotic-looking birds
overlapping the portrait
at the bottom.

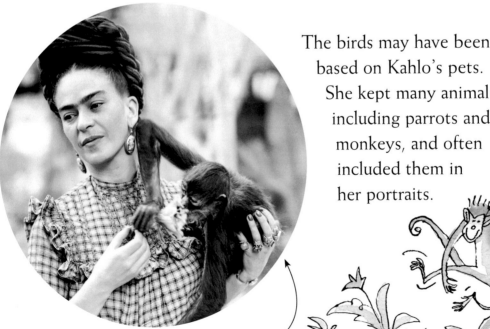

Kahlo with a pet monkey.

The face was painted on metal. Because metal is shiny and doesn't absorb paint, the colors look sharp and strong.

The decorations were painted in see-through colors, on the inside of a piece of glass. This is why the colors change where they overlap the middle.

65

Nighthawks

by Edward Hopper

America, 1942, oil paint on canvas, 33 x 60in (84 x 152cm)

This moody view of a late-night American diner has inspired many other artists, as well as poems, film sets and cartoons.

Lonely nights

Nighthawks are nocturnal birds, and a nickname for people who do things at night, like the characters in this scene. None of them seems to be talking to each other. And the shape of the diner makes them remote from us, cut off by a wall of glass with no visible entrance.

The artist, Edward Hopper, said the picture was inspired by a street corner in New York – but it could be any one of dozens of cities. He captures it looking dark and deserted, and admitted, "unconsciously, probably, I was painting the loneliness of a large city."

Notice the picture's low, wide shape and smooth surface, which make it look like a movie screen. Dramatic, shadowy lighting adds to the movie-like feel.

See how the artist evokes the greenish-yellow glow of fluorescent lights.

This lettering above the diner is part of an advertisement. The diner's name isn't shown — it remains anonymous, like the people inside.

All the figures were based on the artist and his wife, Jo.

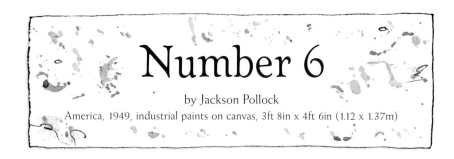

Number 6

by Jackson Pollock

America, 1949, industrial paints on canvas, 3ft 8in x 4ft 6in (1.12 x 1.37m)

American artist Jackson Pollock became famous for his "drip" paintings, made up of tangled webs of lines and splotches of color.

Jack the dripper

To create the drip paintings, Pollock came up with a whole new way of working. He laid his canvas on the floor and dripped, poured and splashed paint over it – earning him the nickname, "Jack the Dripper."

At first glance, it might look messy and random, but Pollock insisted, "There is no accident." When he painted, all his movements were deliberate and controlled. People who saw him said it was like watching a dance, full of energy and rhythm.

What's it all about?

The drip paintings are abstract pictures – meaning they don't try to show any kind of real-life scene. Instead, Pollock created patterns that are also a record of the movements he made while painting – the swooping arcs and sudden splashes. So really, these paintings are about the *action* involved in creating them.

The simple title (just a number) carefully avoids suggesting any particular object or meaning for the picture.

Look for colorful bursts of red, yellow and green beneath the black and white.

See how the lack of any single focus makes your eyes keep moving over the picture surface.

Look for different kinds of marks, from big splotches and bold lines to thin streaks and delicate spatters.

69

70

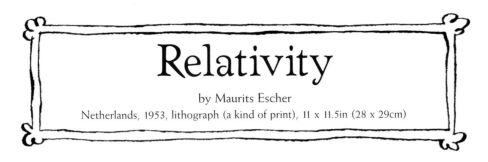

Relativity

by Maurits Escher

Netherlands, 1953, lithograph (a kind of print), 11 x 11.5in (28 x 29cm)

This strange, dreamlike scene was designed about 50 years ago,
as a kind of puzzle. It shows a building full of archways and staircases,
all apparently solid and lifelike – yet full of people walking up
and down at impossible angles to each other.

Which way is up?

The scene is like the meeting of three worlds, each with its own
"up" and "down," so that one person's floor becomes another's
wall, and it becomes impossible to say which way up to look at it.
For centuries, artists have tried to create a sense of real, 3-D space
on flat, 2-D canvases. This picture reminds us that art is an illusion,
and artists can draw unreal scenes as convincingly as real ones.

Notice how the figures all lack faces, adding to the sense of mystery.

Look for dark, shadowy doorways appearing strangely just next to bright, sunlit gardens.

These details show which parts of the scene belong to which "world."

The picture has been built up very precisely, out of neat, black-and-white lines. Notice the delicate use of hatching (crossed lines) to create shading.

Making illusions

The artist, Maurits Escher, was inspired by optical illusions
and mathematical models. You might think the whole structure
is impossible, but in fact you could build a set of staircases that
looked like this – you just couldn't walk up and down them
all together at the same time.

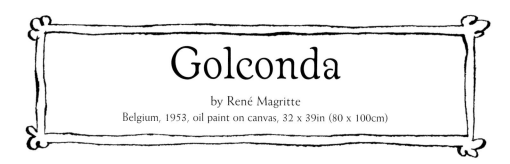

Golconda

by René Magritte

Belgium, 1953, oil paint on canvas, 32 x 39in (80 x 100cm)

This peculiar 1950s painting shows hundreds of men in bowler hats, floating in the sky above an ordinary-looking street, or perhaps raining down onto it. Frequently copied, it has inspired everything from comics to commercials.

Truth and lies

Although this is a strange, dreamlike image, it is presented in a very flat, matter-of-fact way. It is smoothly painted, with lifelike colors and shadows. So if you look at them separately, the individual men and houses appear quite convincing. It is only the combination that makes them seem absurd.

The result is comical, but it is also meant to make us think carefully about art. The artist, René Magritte, said he wanted to challenge the viewer's expectations. His pictures remind us that, however convincing they look, paintings are not real. They are illusions created by the artist, and can lie just as easily as tell the truth.

Notice how the men come in three sizes, each arranged neatly in rows.

At first, the men seem identical and anonymous. But look for little differences, such as how they are posed.

Magritte signed his picture on the wall of the house on the right.

Some people think Magritte based the men on himself. He often wore a dark suit and bowler hat.

74

Fall

by Bridget Riley

England, 1963, emulsion paint on hardboard, 4ft 8in x 4ft 7in (1.41 x 1.40m)

This bold, black-and-white painting uses clever visual effects to explore the experience of seeing. Try staring at the pattern for a while. Do the lines seem to flicker or change? And do you find it hard to keep looking at one spot?

Falling for it

Look for the way the pattern of curves repeats across the picture, creating a sense of recurring rhythms.

Notice how the curves become smaller and tighter as they move downward, giving a feeling of increasing tension.

Very small, subtle variations in the pattern make it constantly seem to shift as you look around it.

The wave-like pattern has a strong downward movement, similar to water in a waterfall – hence the name, *Fall*. And the lack of any central focus encourages your eyes to keep moving around, instead of remaining fixed on one point. So looking at the picture is a constantly changing, unsettling experience.

Optical effects

The picture was finished in 1963 and bought by London's prestigious Tate Gallery the same year. It has since become one of the most famous paintings of the 1960s, and of the movement sometimes known as "Op" art. Op is the name given to art that exploits the way our eyes work.

The paint surface is so smooth and precise, you can't see any brushmarks or flaws, even in close up.

75

Marilyn

by Andy Warhol

America, 1967, screenprint on paper, 36 x 36in (92 x 92cm)

American artist Andy Warhol was fascinated with the idea of fame. He created colorful images of many celebrities, including this print of movie star Marilyn Monroe. In fact, he made hundreds of "Marilyn" prints – prints which in turn helped to assure his own fame as an artist.

Notice how few colors there are; the number was restricted by the printing process.

Look for the way patches of color overlap or even miss the edges of shapes.

Flawed features

Marilyn's face fills the frame, a bright, bold image of a famous star. But there is something deliberately crude about it, too. The shapes and colors have been hugely simplified, and the printing process has left obvious flaws. Seen like this, the star's famous features start to look flat and unreal, suggesting a darker side to fame. In fact, Warhol was inspired to start making the prints by Marilyn's death a few years earlier.

The print is part of a series of ten, showing Marilyn in varying colors.

Mass-produced prints

Warhol based all his "Marilyn" prints on a single publicity photograph. He made the prints in an unusually mechanical way. Calling his studio "The Factory," he used modern printing techniques and numerous assistants to set up a kind of assembly line, churning out copies. Some people think this kind of "mass-produced" image is less artistic than a traditional painting. But Warhol wanted to challenge tradition.

Mr. and Mrs. Clark and Percy

by David Hockney

England, 1970-71, acrylic paint on canvas, 7 x 10ft (2.13 x 3.04m)

This double portrait shows a glamorous couple, fashion designers Celia Birtwell and Ossie Clark, at home in London. The artist, David Hockney, was a close friend and painted this as a wedding gift.

Painted relationship

The scattered objects and Ossie's slouching, barefoot pose give the picture a deceptively casual look. But it was all carefully arranged, with lots of strong geometric shapes and the couple posed symmetrically on either side of a window.

Hockney spent most of a year on the picture, saying his goal was: "to paint the relationship of these two people." To show Celia standing and Ossie sitting was deliberately unconventional; in a traditional portrait, the man would stand. And the gap between the two hints at tension. In fact, the couple were to separate a few years later.

Look for the way the light coming from the window behind throws everything into sharp relief, creating strong outlines and making shapes look flatter.

In real life, the figures in the painting are nearly life size, which was a huge challenge for the artist. He made lots of preparatory sketches and painted Ossie's head twelve times before he was satisfied.

The white cat was actually named Blanche, but Hockney put Percy (the name of the couple's other cat) in the title, because he thought it sounded better.

Notice how Celia and Ossie both gaze in the same direction. It's as if they are looking back out of the picture at you, or at the artist painting them.

Index

abstract, 55, 56, 68
America, 56, 59, 66, 68, 77
American Gothic, 58-59
Arnolfini Portrait, 8-9
Austria, 48
Bar at the Folies, 38-39
Belgium, 8, 72
Blue Dancers, 44-45
Botticelli, 10
color contrasts, 40, 45, 50
Courtyard of a House, 22-23
Dalí, 60
Dance at the Moulin, 36-37
De Hooch, 23
Degas, 45
dreams, 61, 71, 72
England, 28, 32, 34, 75, 78
Escher, 71
Fall, 74-75
Fighting Temeraire, 32-33
France, 37, 38, 45, 52
fresco, 16
Gainsborough, 28
Girl with a Pearl Earring, 26-27
Golconda, 72-73
Great Wave, 30-31

Guernica, 62-63
Harmony in Red, 50-51
Hockney, 78
Hokusai, 30
Hopper, 66
illusion, 23, 50, 71, 72
Italy, 10, 13, 14, 16
Japan, 30
Kahlo, 64
Kandinsky, 54
Kiss, 48-49
Klimt, 48
landscape, 29
Leonardo, 14
Magritte, 72
Maids of Honor, 20-21
Manet, 38, 39
Marilyn, 76-77
Matisse, 50
Mexico, 64
Michelangelo, 16, 17
Millais, 34
Mona Lisa, 14-15
Monet, 52, 53
Mr. and Mrs. Andrews, 28-29
Mr. and Mrs. Clark, 78-79

Munch, 47
myths and stories, 10, 13
Netherlands, 23, 25, 26, 43, 71
Nighthawks, 66-67
Number 6, 68-69
O'Keeffe, 56
Ophelia, 34-35
Oriental Poppies, 56-57
paints,
  acrylic paint, 78
  emulsion paint, 75
  industrial paint, 68
  oil paint, 8, 13, 14, 21, 23, 25, 26,
    28, 32, 34, 37, 38, 40, 43, 45, 47,
    48, 50, 52, 54, 56, 59, 60, 62, 64,
    66, 72
  tempera paint, 10, 47
  watercolor paint, 16
patterns, 48, 49, 50, 51, 75
Persistence of Memory, 60-61
perspective, 15, 23
Picasso, 62, 63
Pollock, 68
portraits, 8-9, 14-15, 20-21, 26-27,
  28-29, 78-79
  self portraits, 8, 16, 24-25, 43, 64-65

prints, 30, 71, 77
Raphael, 13
Relativity, 70-71
Rembrandt, 25
Renoir, 37
Riley, 75
Russia, 54
Scream, 46-47
Seurat, 40
Sistine Chapel, 16-19
Spain, 21, 60, 62, 63
Spring, 10-11
St. George and the Dragon, 12-13
Sunday on La Grande Jatte, 40-41
Sunflowers, 42-43
symbols and symbolic meanings, 8,
  9, 35, 43, 60, 61
Turner, 32
Van Eyck, 8
Van Gogh, 43
Velásquez, 21
Vermeer, 26
Warhol, 77
Water Lilies, 52-53
Wood, 59
Yellow – Red – Blue, 54-55

Acknowledgements

Picture research by Ruth King. Edited by Jane Chisholm & Jenny Tyler. American editor: Carrie Armstrong. Cover design by Mary Cartwright. Additional illustrations by Emily Bornoff. Every effort has been made to trace the copyright holders of the material in this book. If any rights have been omitted, the publishers offer their sincere apologies and will rectify this in any subsequent editions following notification. The publishers are grateful to the following organisations and individuals for their contributions and permission to reproduce material: Cover: see credits for pages 14-15 & 30-31. Page 1: see credit for pages 20-21. Pages 2-3: see credit for pages 52-53. Pages 6-7: see credit for pages 42-43. Pages 8-9: **Arnolfini Portrait** © National Gallery, London. Man in a Turban © National Gallery, London. Pages 10-11: **Spring** (Uffizi Gallery, Florence) © Summerfield Press/Corbis. Pages 12-13: **St. George & the Dragon** © Louvre Museum, Paris/Giraudon/Bridgeman Art Library. Pages 14-15: **Mona Lisa** (Louvre Museum, Paris) © Gianni Dagli Orti/Corbis. Pages 16-17: **Creation of Adam** (Vatican Museums & Galleries, Vatican City, Rome) © Gallery Collection/Corbis. **Last Judgement** (detail) © Vatican Museums & Galleries, Vatican City/Alinari/Bridgeman Art Library. Pages 18-19: **Sistine Chapel ceiling** © Vatican Museums & Galleries, Vatican City/Bridgeman Art Library. Pages 20-21: **Maids of Honor** © Photo Scala, Florence/Prado Museum, Madrid. Pages 22-23: **Courtyard of a House** © National Gallery, London. Pages 24-25: Rembrandt **Self Portrait** © Iveagh Bequest, Kenwood House, London/Bridgeman Art Library. Pages 26-27: **Girl with a Pearl Earring** (Mauritshuis, Hague) © Francis G. Mayer/Corbis. Pages 28-29: **Mr. & Mrs. Andrews** © National Gallery, London. Pages 30-31: **Great Wave** (copies in many museums, including **Metropolitan Museum, New York** & **British Museum, London**) © Historical Picture Archive/Corbis. Pages 32-33: "**Fighting Temeraire**" © National Gallery, London. Pages 34-35: **Ophelia** © Art Archive/Tate Gallery, London/Eileen Tweedy. Pages 36-37: **Dance at the Moulin** © Orsay Museum, Paris/Giraudon/Bridgeman Art Library. Pages 38-39: **Bar at the Folies** © Samuel Courtauld Trust, **Courtauld Institute of Art Gallery, London**/Bridgeman Art Library. Pages 40-41: **Sunday on La Grande Jatte** (Art Institute of Chicago) © Gallery Collection/Corbis. Pages 42-43: **Sunflowers** © Philadelphia Museum of Art/Corbis. Van Gogh **Self Portrait** © Samuel Courtauld Trust, **Courtauld Institute of Art Gallery, London**/ Bridgeman Art Library. Pages 44-45: **Blue Dancers** (Orsay Museum, Paris) © Art Archive/Corbis. Pages 46-47: **Scream** © National Museum of Art, Architecture & Design, Oslo/Munch Museum/Munch-Ellingsen Group, BONO, Oslo/DACS, London 2009; photo: Jacques Lathion. Pages 48-49: **Kiss** (Belvedere, Vienna) © Photo Austrian Archive/Scala, Florence. Pages 50-51: **Harmony in Red** (Hermitage Museum, St. Petersburg) © Succession H. Matisse/DACS 2009; photo: Archives Matisse. Pages 52-53: **Waterlilies** © Orangerie Museum, Paris/ Lauros/Giraudon/Bridgeman Art Library. Photo of Giverny © Steven Vidler/Eurasia Press/Corbis. Pages 54-55: **Yellow - Red - Blue** © National Museum of Modern Art, Paris/Peter Willi/ Bridgeman Art Library/ADAGP, Paris & DACS, London 2009. Pages 56-57: **Oriental Poppies** © Collection of Frederick R. Weisman Museum at University of Minnesota, Minneapolis; Museum Purchase/Georgia O'Keeffe Museum/DACS, London 2009. Pages 58-59: **American Gothic** © Art Institute of Chicago/Bridgeman Art Library//All Rights Reserved by the Estate of Nan Wood Graham/Licensed by VAGA, New York, NY. Photo of house © Tom Bean/Corbis. Pages 60-61: **Persistence of Memory** © Digital image, **Museum of Modern Art, New York**/Scala, Florence; © Salvador Dali, Gala-Salvador Dali Foundation/DACS, London 2009. Pages 62-63: **Guernica** © Queen Sofia Museum, Madrid/Bridgeman Art Library/Succession Picasso/DACS, London 2009. Photo of Guernica © Bettmann/Corbis. Pages 64-65: **Self Portrait/The Frame** (National Museum of Modern Art, Paris) © INBA, Mexico & 2009 Banco de Mexico Diego Rivera & Frida Kahlo Museum Trust, Mexico D.F./DACS, London 2009; photo © Photo CNAC/MNAM, Dist. RMN/Jean-Claude Planchet. Photo of Kahlo © Bettmann/ Corbis. Pages 66-67: **Nighthawks** (Art Institute of Chicago) © Francis G. Mayer/Corbis. Pages 68-69: **Number 6** © Museum of Fine Arts, Houston/D. & J. de Menil Fund/Bridgeman Art Library/Pollock-Krasner Foundation/ARS, New York & DACS, London 2009. Pages 70-71: **Relativity** (copies in many museums, including **Metropolitan Museum, New York**) © 2008 M.C. Escher Company-Holland; All Rights Reserved; www.mcescher.com. Pages 72-73: **Golconda** © Menil Collection, Houston/Lauros/Giraudon/Bridgeman Art Library/ADAGP, Paris & DACS, London 2009. Pages 74-75: **Fall** (Tate Modern, London) © 2009 Bridget Riley; All Rights Reserved. Pages 76-77: **Marilyn** (copies in many museums, including **Museum of Modern Art, New York**) © Andy Warhol Foundation/Corbis. Pages 78-79: **Mr. & Mrs. Clark & Percy** © David Hockney; digital image © **Tate Gallery, London** 2009.

Usborne Publishing Ltd has paid DACS' visual creators for the use of their artistic works.